BUILDING SUCCESSFUL DESIGN THINKING TEAMS

SUCCESSFULLY DESIGNING AGILE INNOVATION FOR COMPANIES AND ORGANIZATIONS

ANNA S. LINK

Contents

Foreword

Design thinking seems to be the method of choice, especially in the German-speaking world, when it comes to innovation and agile product conception. No matter whether it is software, hardware, services or entire business plans. Take "Design Thinking" and it seems to be guaranteed that breakthrough innovations will be achieved and the whole competition will be overtaken. But is this really the case?

Not least due to the influence and activities of SAP co-founder Hasso Plattner and the institute named after him, Design Thinking seems to be unstoppable. In the process, a very specific form and interpretation of design thinking is presented, which is by no means the only one and deviates in some aspects from those of the original forms.

Many books have been written about Design Thinking and there are also many about approaches such as Design Sprint (a form of Design Thinking known from the Google environment, for example) or about completely different agile innovation methods such as Lego(R) Serious Play(R) and many others.

This book has a different focus than conventional design thinking books. It is not about reproducing a multitude of methods. There are plenty of books for that, some with hundreds of methods. Particularly recommended here is "Das große Handbuch Innovation" from the Vahlen publishing house, which presents 555 methods and tools.

The aim of this book is rather to convey the necessary mindset with regard to the introduction, structure and design of Design Thinking. In particular, it also deals with the requirements for setting up Design Thinking teams and the framework conditions that support the successful implementation of Design Thinking and the optimal achievement of goals.

I wish you much success with your Design Thinking Challenge!

The author

CHAPTER ONE

Introduction to Design Thinking

Design Thinking is a framework that has become increasingly important in recent years. Due to the changes in the business world towards a reality characterized by VUCA (Volatility - Uncertainty - Complexity - Ambiguity), where changes often happen within weeks and months and not within years or decades, new requirements also arise. The market and its influences and needs have become increasingly diverse and complex. The time of top experts who can find the next product generations or solutions for upcoming problems on their own from their ivory tower, so to speak, is over. The pace of change is far too fast and the number of influencing factors to be taken into account is far too large. Only through the synergetic cooperation of people with the most diverse experience and knowledge is it still possible to survive on the market in the long term.

In this context, approaches such as Design Thinking, Design Sprint or Lean UX, but also a variety of other approaches such as Lego ® Serious Play ® have proven their worth. In this book, I will focus on Design Thinking, but recommend that you also get to know alternative tools and approaches and check them for possible use in the context of your questions.

Design thinking is an approach that goes back to the three Stanford professors Terry Winograd, Larry Leifer and David Kelley and focuses on people and their needs. User-centeredness is the central principle of Design Thinking. The benefit for the user / customer / user is in the foreground of the concepts and products developed with Design Thinking. The first question that Design Thinking addresses is always that of the user's needs. Technological feasibility and economic viability are only addressed subsequently, but are of course of great importance for an implementation decision.

As a true agile method, design thinking is based on an approach that states that the synergy of people with a wide variety of experiences and competencies creates a better and more goal-oriented solution than would be possible through individual specialists.

Design thinking has long since been used not only for the creation of innovative products and services. It represents a fundamental approach with which problems and questions from the most diverse contexts can be processed in a structured manner. The area of application includes product development, service development, process design, but also the development of entire corporate strategies. The multi-perspective view of the problem brought in by the various participants supports this.

Another typical agile approach is the iterative approach of design thinking. Here, you move through the process step by step, learn as you go, and can go back to earlier steps if it turns out that an approach does not achieve the desired goals. We are therefore moving here in a process model that is based on experimental development. Here, errors are not perceived as something negative, but as a central requirement of the development process. Schools and organizations in the context of Design Thinking assume different phase models with a different number of steps. However, this does not mean that completely different approaches are used, but rather that different schools group the corresponding activities and questions differently and sometimes also weight them.

CHAPTER TWO

A Design Thinking Phase Model

For the presentation in this book, I assume a phase model as it is used in Germany, for example, by the Hasso Plattner Institute and a large number of trainers and experts trained there.

The model is based on a clearly structured concept. The six phases of the model are first divided into the problem space and the solution space. Both spaces comprise three phases each. While the problem space is about evaluating and understanding the problem or issue, the solution space is about developing solutions. In addition, both spaces are based on a diverging approach, in which more information and insights are to be gained, and on a converging part, in which the information and insights gained are in turn sifted, evaluated and concretized.

Within the different phases, a wide variety of methods can be used, depending on the problem and the team composition. There are books that offer hundreds of methods and approaches. Of course, not all of them have to be used and many of them have never been used even by experienced design thinkers. In fact, Design Thinking is not so much about methods and theories, but more about "doing it" and maintaining a healthy critical faculties towards the gained results, to question them and - if the gain of knowledge is not sufficient - to pursue other methods and approaches. The goal is always the realization of benefits for the customer, and this can look very different, just like the way to achieve it.

Basically, one must keep in mind: The method and the process are more or less the basis, the implementation in everyday life. However, this in turn is based on an attitude that harmonizes with the principles of Design Thinking and expresses itself through a certain type of collaboration with employees and customers. Without a corresponding attitude, Design

Thinking, like every agile method and every agile framework, is not powerful, but at best a collection of new methods and techniques, whose usefulness, however, is considerably limited.

Behind this is a certain culture that is lived in the organization. We are not talking here about any external marketing statements aimed at winning over customers, but about the lived basis for activities, statements and cooperation within the organization itself and within the organization with its various stakeholders. We will discuss this topic in more detail in later sections.

In the following, let us run through a Design Thinking process using a concrete Design Thinking Challenge as an example. The methods used are, of course, only a selection from many equally applicable possibilities. We will use the following example (due to the current situation during the creation of the book):

Re-design of a collaboration in teams in a situation where parts of the team are often not present at the same location for a longer period of time, but for example work in a home office or have their place of work in other branches or even countries ("distributed teams").

Understand

In the "Understanding" step, a common idea of what problem / challenge needs to be solved is to be developed. The aim is to understand the various problem dimensions, to make the participants aware of and share their assumptions, and to create motivation in the team to find a good solution to the named problem.

Team members often find it difficult to really focus on the problem and not immediately go into finding a solution. Important aspects are often lost in the process. Although it can be assumed that the team members have a rough idea of the problem, are all the important points really known to everyone involved? Does the team's idea of the problem also correspond to that of the customer? Are all participants also aware of what is part of the problem for the customer and what is not? Far too often, without a clear picture, solutions are only found for partial aspects or aspects that are important for the customer are not addressed at all. Solution approaches are then based only on one's own experiences and points of view and may not be of any use to the customer, or only to a limited extent.

Every Design Thinking project starts with a Design Challenge. As already mentioned, we will approach our further considerations based on a concrete challenge. This is as follows:

Re-design of a collaboration in teams in a situation where parts of the team are often not present at the same location for a longer period of time, but for example work in a home office or have their place of work in other branches or even countries ("distributed teams").

A useful first step is for the team to jointly determine which statements/ information from the Challenge need to be looked at more closely. It is important that we work with an interdisciplinary team with a wide range of experience and knowledge in order to incorporate synergies from all possible perspectives and to consider the question as holistically as possible.

A good tool that is often used at the beginning of a challenge is called "semantic analysis". It comes from the field of linguistics. In this process, the different members gather their associations to the different components of the statement. In this phase, we want to gather as wide a range of different viewpoints as possible, so that we can also find and record viewpoints and aspects that are not obvious at first glance.

Based on our example, it could be useful, for example, to take a closer look at terms such as "team collaboration", "home office", "collaboration with other branches/locations", "cross-border collaboration". This can be done, for example, by having the team members write their associations with the various terms on individual moderation cards or sticky notes or, if necessary, sketch them; these are then grouped into the various terms and statements.

For example, regarding the term "home office," statements such as "disruption by roommates," "no traffic jams on the way to work," "loneliness," "not being up to date," "work time control," "life/work balance," etc. could be recorded.

Once we have worked out a joint overview of the various aspects and viewpoints, it can be useful, depending on the issue, to take a closer look at the people / users / stakeholders affected by the challenge and their needs. A very suitable tool for this is a design charrette (charrette, French = "cart"). Three columns are used. The first is labeled "User, Person or Stakeholder", the second is used to record the assumed needs of the entries in the first column, and the third is used to record the topics that need to be investigated further (for example, in the form of an interview).

When defining the users in the first column, it is a good idea to also get inspiration from "extreme users", i.e. possibly users who have a very special need or requirement associated with the Challenge. This could be, for example, people who are not able to drive to work every day due to health problems, or single parents who have small children and perhaps only have a very limited space to retreat. Another user group may include people who are not only not present in the office, but may be in other locations due to their professional activities, where, for example, the connection to telephone and Internet is not permanently ensured to a sufficient extent. Another possible user group could be colleagues who work in another part of the world and may have night off during the "main team's" usual working hours.

If we think we have identified a large number of relevant users (we can add to this later if necessary), then we move to the middle column. Here we look for each user's needs in the first column. To make it more personal, we can put the needs in the form of quotes. This supports an empathic perception. For example, it could be put in the mouth of the colleague "from the other side of the planet": "When I'm working and have questions, no one is ever available for direct consultation." He could also say, "I often have difficulty dealing with the directness of statements from colleagues from other countries, we have a very different form of communication there" ...

Over time, statements may appear for the various user groups that occur several times or complement each other. Here it may be useful to note such statements in the third column, because it may be worthwhile to examine and question them more closely. Here, we must not fall into the trap of taking our assumptions about users' statements, which may be our assumptions or may correspond to one-time statements in a specific situation, as absolute. Statements, which are important for our further work, must be questioned later in any case in a suitable form. Interviews, for example, could be used for this purpose in a later phase. For this purpose, we collect the topics in the third column.

Observe

In the observation phase, the focus is on the user and his needs. After we have made many assumptions about the user and his needs in the first phase (understanding), it is now a matter of verifying (or falsifying) these. The focus here is not on the desire to be "right", but on achieving the most correct possible assessment of the user, even if this may differ from our assumptions from the first phase. We can ideally implement this if we now compare the topics developed in the design charrette with reality.

In this phase, we want to build empathy for the users and properly understand them and their needs. In doing so, it may well be that through discussions with different users we also come across contradictory or conflicting needs and ideas, which we need to look at more closely. To achieve this, it is necessary to actively engage with users. In doing so, we often find that the user is not really or fully aware of his needs. It is often much easier for him to say what he does not want than what he does want.

When we practice Design Thinking, we will very quickly realize that the "average user" often assumed in quantitative market research by means of questionnaires and similar techniques does not exist at all. This is only a mathematical approximation, which should help us to reduce complexity, but which also leads to the fact that many individual opinions fall through the "statistical grid". There are people with very different needs, knowledge, abilities, who may have very different ideas and experiences in the context of our challenge. In order to finally build innovative solutions in a process that offer real added value and stand out from the average offer in the market, we have to build empathy with our users and understand them. This is not possible with statistical average users, but with people with individual personalities.

For this reason, we contact users directly to find out their stories. Again, there are many different methods for this. In my experience, the most effective is the direct conversation in the form of an interview. Unlike a questionnaire, it offers the possibility of responding individually to unexpected answers and thus possibly obtaining important and inspiring additional information. Unlike questionnaire approaches, a goal-oriented interview is not about working out standardized questions and procedures, but rather about preparing how to tune the interviewee into the topics and motivate him or her to provide answers that are useful for us, where we can follow up if necessary, where in-depth topics could lie, and so on.

Good interviews have their own dramaturgy. A successful approach presented by various authors and schools is the following:

- Addressing and presenting the goal/project (What is it actually about and what is the goal?)

- Building a human relationship (helping the other person to feel comfortable in the conversation and to speak freely - we don't want to work through a questionnaire, we want to have a conversation and share in our other person's experiences and insights in relation to our question)
- Asking for stories / experiences / insights related to our question.
- Discover the emotions behind them and ask questions to clarify or understand the background.
- Conclude the conversation and thank your counterpart for their support.

It is very important to ask open questions. Those who ask closed questions are looking for confirmation or contradiction of their thesis. Those who ask open questions, on the other hand, have the opportunity to gain further insights and possibly find the actual question or topic. It is important to give the other person enough time to let stories develop. To do this, we should listen attentively and let the other person speak, but also allow pauses in which the interlocutor reflects or remembers. When asking questions, be careful that you do not suggest a specific answer with your question and thus reduce your gain in knowledge and the benefit of the conversation.

You probably know the following example from your own experience. You have eaten somewhere and afterwards the host or a member of the service staff comes to your table and asks, "Did you like it?" If you are not in the throes of nausea at the time, you will probably agree in some form and the questioner will leave the table. The very nature of his question has shown you what answer he actually expects. But how would you have answered if he had asked an open-ended question, such as, "We want to continuously improve our performance. Would you have one or two more ideas about what we could do to make your stay with us more enjoyable next time?" - It is also possible that you would have simply said, "It was all good." However, many of those addressed would have realized that what was being asked for here was not confirmation but real input, and they might have offered real concerns and suggestions for improvement. In addition, they might have felt especially valued because their counterpart apparently cares about what they think and what matters to them. This is exactly what we want: to get our conversation partners to give us new points of view. To do this, it is necessary for our interlocutor to perceive themselves as an important partner, not as an interview partner who is being "worked through".

It is always worthwhile to practice such interviews as a team first and to give each other feedback. Make sure to always conduct interviews in pairs. Then one person can concentrate on the interview and the other can take appropriate notes and also give the other person feedback after the interview, which can help them to further improve their interview technique. Be sure to discuss the interview with the interviewee after the interview as a team of two as well. Often one or the other overhears a statement or there are different perceptions. Record the important issues accordingly. Aspects for documentation could be:

- Description of the person
- Interesting quotes and statements
- Things that surprised or may need further clarification
- Things that have particularly inspired or raised new aspects
- Further

It could be, for example, that a colleague from an overseas branch tells us that at a certain point in time he had found an error that could have caused significant problems with the delivery scheduled for the next day but, due to the different time zones, he had not been able to reach anyone and the team had therefore traveled to the customer in vain to carry out the installation.

You will find that you will get very different information, which may also contradict each other. This is because you have interviewed people with different personalities and needs and there is no such thing as a "standard customer", only people with different wishes and requirements.

Once we have conducted enough interviews to gain a broader understanding, we can use this to move into the synthesis phase.

Define synthesis

Now that we have worked to understand the problem and the question and to verify our conclusions, for example by means of interviews, the next step is to define a common view. Note: We are still in the problem space at this stage. So it is not yet a matter of already agreeing on or developing approaches to a solution.

This phase is characterized by the team playing together with the data they find, recombining it, interpreting it in a variety of ways, and working to identify common patterns. This work is done as a team. In the process, the various observations made are questioned and it is jointly determined what relevance is assigned to them.

We want to work out together which user needs have been found. The idea is to decide together which of the identified needs are relevant enough that it would be worthwhile to look for solutions for them. These kinds of user needs will later form the basis for inspirations for new solutions.

The tools in the synthesis phase are also called frameworks or templates. The term template comes from the fact that this phase is about presenting and interpreting the existing data in different ways. When working with templates, it is always important that they are used and processed jointly in the team in order to include different points of view and backgrounds of experience. There are dozens of methods and techniques that can be used in the context of the synthesis phase. We will focus on a few in the following. The techniques presented are not better than others; rather, in the context of issues and teams, it is always a matter of selecting and using the ideal tools for the specific case and the intended benefit.

A very simple approach that is often used is based on storytelling. Instead of exchanging any protocols or lists in the team as results of the conducted conversations, the interviewers tell the stories that emerged in the conducted conversations. The focus is not so much on a complete reproduction of all details, but on the information and content that is likely to inspire the team and give them new insights. Important points here are:

- The interlocutor - it is not about the biographical data, but about conveying the perceived person and making it palpable for the other team members.
- The needs that were expressed in relation to our question.
- The circumstances or situations in which the stated needs occur or are of particular importance to the interlocutor.

The interviewers tell the other team members about the interviews conducted. Each interview is discussed and replayed separately. Important quotes from the interview partner are also particularly meaningful. The other team members listen attentively and note down their findings on separate moderation cards or sticky notes. Caution: It may well be that an interviewee expresses completely different needs in different situations and circumstances. For example, in the context of home office, someone may say that he or she would very much like to have opportunities for informal exchange within the team during the day; on the other hand, the same person may also say that it is also important to him or her to be able to work in a very focused and concentrated manner, and accordingly needs times when he or she is not contacted. The moderation cards or sticky notes are hung on a moderation wall. It is helpful to cluster statements from one person based on different topic areas, especially if there are a larger number of findings.

The participants will now reflect on the statements and each participant will select one that seems to be of particular interest or particularly meaningful. It may be that this is related to the fact that existing assumptions are questioned as a result or that additional aspects have been added or similar. The relevant statements are highlighted separately and the reason for the choice is attached with a keyword as a reminder. The various parties involved will usually highlight very different aspects in the process.

Now the task is to extract new, previously unknown information and correlations from the data obtained. A good way to do this is to use a 2x2 matrix, in which the two axes correspond to two attributes or characteristics evident in the data, which are represented in the two axes. Thus, in our example, one axis could represent the work situation in terms of "working in peace, undisturbed" and "working in a team, interactively", whereas the second dimension could possibly represent the need for social contact. The previously jointly named statements with special meaning can now be positioned in the matrix to see if this possibly results in new insights or assumptions. Of course, several matrices with different characteristics and attributes can be used to trace completely different possible connections. Some will yield more information, others may yield little or none.

Another possibility that can help us gain additional insights is to pick out particularly important aspects. Which personality is hidden behind this and can we possibly gain further insights from it? It is important that we do not portray our interviewees from the interviews, but develop a persona. This personifies, so to speak, the data that we have obtained in the course of various interviews. It helps to give the persona a name and to formulate some additional attributes such as profession, life situation, family, age, wishes and goals as well as, depending on the context, questions such as which media the persona uses. The important thing here is to create a persona that generates empathy, not overdrawn caricatures. Only in this way can a persona evoke identification and inspiration. In some projects and contexts, such personas are so strong that they accompany the team for a long time and become more and more concrete for the team members over time.

Another method in the context of synthesis is the formulation of a Point of View. The structure is similar to what some people know as a user story, for example in the context of Scrum. The structure is:

As a <user>, I have a specific <need> in a specific <context>.

One also often finds the following formulation for clarification:

"Our user <name> has a need for <need> in a world where <context> exists."

To make this more concrete, we can choose a formulation in the context of our example situation:

As a home office employee, I like to maintain informal communication with colleagues during work hours when I can't be in the office for extended periods of time.

A sentence formulated jointly in this way can once again condense the view in the team and support a common understanding. If the statement formulated in this way is meaningful and useful for the entire team, it can decide to enter the solution space with it. The Redesign Challenge has been concretized to such an extent that we can proceed to the development of solution approaches based on it. This may mean that some aspects will be dropped and not pursued further for the moment. It may be that, based on the experience gained in the further process, we will return to them.

Exercise for creating a persona

There are different approaches to developing a persona. Some organizations have standard personas that are meant to represent the various target customer groups, others have created personas needed in the context of specific projects or product developments. In the following, I would like to present an approach I like very much, which originally goes back to Christopher Daniels, Sr. Experience Designer at Adobe, and has been slightly adapted by me.

Personas, as we want to use them - often also referred to as proto-personas - represent our best guess as to who uses (or will use) our products and why he or she does so. These are not real people, but virtual people defined on the basis of experience, analysis and assumptions, which help us to develop products for "people" rather than "abstract customers". After all, people have different needs, motivations, and access to markets and information.

Alan Cooper, the "father of Visual Basic," testified about personas that it is more important that a persona be precise rather than exact. That is, it is more important to define the persona in great detail and specificity than to be the exact match.

Now let's go through an example process together to develop personas for our product or service.

1. Identification and segmentation: determine who will use the product

- Record all the people who are currently using the product or will use it in the future. Attention: It may be that there are completely different uses.
- Keep each user on a separate sticky note
- Identify common and different characteristics of different users and group them accordingly

2. Attributes and profiling: Form clusters of "like" users

- Record the answers to the following questions on different colored sticky notes depending on the question:

  - Define basic demographic data for each type of user group: Gender, age, education level ...
  - Define needs, wishes and goals for the different user groups. Sentence starters such as "I have to", "I need" or "I want" can be helpful for this.
  - Define the pain points of the different user groups. You can use sentence starters like "I find it difficult", "It frustrates me that/if" or similar.
  - Define the requirements for the product/service for the different user groups. What does the product need to do/provide to make users happy/successful?

- Consolidate the corresponding attributes.

3. Spectrum profiling: describe the types of people who use the product/service using a spectrum and define common, average, and dominant characteristics.

- For each group, identify 5-10 attributes that you think are important/meaningful and name the extremes, e.g., "experienced user" versus "new user" or "infrequent user" versus "frequent user"
- For the different group members, record their positioning on the different spectra (for example, using different color dots)
- Discuss the observations: Can patterns be discerned or do they seem random?
- Consolidate the values per group and attribute. Where no pattern can be seen, the corresponding attribute may not be significant for a group.

4. Personification: Create prototypical personas from the groups

- From your insights from each group, generate a persona that represents their consolidated attributes.
- Make the personas into people by giving them names and other attributes that help build empathy. A picture is helpful for this. (Caution: Do not use images with which you may have a previous experience, such as real people in their environment or celebrities, as this could lead to distortions).
- Add typical statements to the persona
- Record each persona on an individual document and post it so that all team members have it "in front of them" at all times.

Find ideas

With the phase "Finding ideas" we step from the problem space - where it was about analyzing the problem in more detail and thus ensuring that we work on the problems that are also of importance and benefit - into the solution space. Here, the focus is on finding one or more solutions to the problem we previously worked on together. The solution space also consists of three phases. In the following phases, the focus is now on finding as many solution approaches as possible (finding ideas), presenting them prototypically (generating prototypes) and finally testing them with users (testing).

In the "Finding ideas" phase, the aim is to generate as many ideas as possible that could solve the user's problem. So we are again in a phase where the aim is to generate quantity, which we will then scrutinize and thin out again in the subsequent phases. A variety of methods are available for this purpose, which can all essentially be summarized under the keyword "brainstorming". The goal of generating as many ideas as possible does not mean that the quality of the ideas is not important, but rather that it is often not even possible to clearly define in advance which ideas are good and which are not. Often, this only becomes apparent in the course of further investigations. In addition, an impractical idea can also lead to a team member being inspired and thus having his or her own goal-oriented idea derived from it.

Three basic principles should apply at this stage:

1. No criticism of ideas
2. Building on the ideas of others - thinking ahead to the ideas of others
3. Encourage "wild" ideas - those that don't fit at first glance or seem a bit "crazy".

We now take needs formulated in the synthesis and formulate them as questions:

- "How can we ... realize?"
- "How can we ... solve the problem?"
- a. o.

Now the team can concentrate on the specific question.

Methods that can be used in this context are all forms of brainstorming: classic brainstorming, brainstorming paradox, silent brainstorming or similar. In addition, approaches such as the Walt Disney method, the 6-hats method or many others can also be used here. One way of looking at topics from a completely different perspective can be a change of perspective, for example, in which the team looks at the issue from the point of view of different personalities or characters:

- What would Elon Musk do?
- How would Pipi Longstocking react?

- What would Harry Potter's solution be?
- How would Gandhi deal with the challenge?
- etc.

When selecting the methods, the team in question and the personalities of its members should be taken into account. If, for example, there are introverted members in the team, approaches in which idea-finding processes are carried out individually and the ideas found are then brought together may be more effective in obtaining contributions from all team members.

Once initial ideas have been formulated, it can be helpful if each team member formulates further ideas based on them. A frequently used approach is the 6-3-5 method. In a team of six (6), each team member formulates one idea on a sheet in three columns (3). This sheet is then given in turn to the other 5 team members, who in turn formulate a continuation per idea, which is based on the original idea. Alternatively, all ideas of the other team members that have been entered in the column so far can also be included. This results in a total of 90 ideas. If the team does not consist of six members, but of 7, for example, 7-3-6 or, in the case of 8, 8-3-7 is also conceivable. For even larger teams, a division into two groups should be considered. For the generation of an idea, a time limit of, for example, 45-60 seconds should be chosen so that the whole thing happens as spontaneously as possible. Alternatively, more time can be allowed if the goal is further elaboration of one's idea instead of simple brainstorming.

A selection must then be made from the large number of ideas generated using the methods mentioned or other methods. Various points of view can be decisive in this selection. Criteria could be:

- Especially innovative and wild ideas
- Ideas which can be implemented quickly and/or cost-effectively
- Ideas which users particularly like

The selection can be made in a team, for example, with the help of sticky dots (for example, in different colors, based on the selected criteria). The idea with the most points is then carried over to the next phase and worked on further there.

Generate prototypes

In the subsequent "Generate prototypes" phase, an initial version of a product or service is created. The aim here is to put the idea into shape in such a way that potential users can experience, test and evaluate it. So the goal is always to be able to determine whether we are on the right track with our idea. The "generate prototypes" phase is accordingly a concretization of "find ideas" and a preliminary stage of "test", where the developed prototypes are tested. The goal here is to gain additional insights with little effort.

We build prototypes to create additional understanding within the team and on the other hand to create a basis for deeper communication with our users, which allows to create increased understanding through feedback.

When we generate prototypes, for example, we can first build simple elements - which help us verify assumptions about the customer's needs - and then build further based on the corresponding feedback, gradually approaching a solution.

Based on the individual understanding of the ideas formulated in the ideation phase, team members are each asked to independently create prototypes. These results are then brought to the table together and used to synergistically generate further prototypes and prototypes based on them. Different materials are suitable for generating prototypes, depending on the issue. Here is a small selection:

- Lego sets/Playmobil or similar.
- Styrofoam molds
- Craft materials
- Wool ball/binding thread
- Paper, cardboard, post-its
- Tools
- Wooden blocks
- Fabric
- Materials from nature: branches, leaves, stones
- a. o.
- Of course, prototypes can also be implemented with technical approaches, PC, 3D printer or similar

Once a reasonable number of prototypes have been created, the team decides which prototypes should be further developed and tested by users. A joint prototype is now built to be presented to users.

Experience shows that prototypes that are too elaborate and look too perfect often discourage users from giving honest feedback. The solutions appear as if nothing more can be done to them and an infinite amount of effort has already been put into them, while prototypes that do not look quite so perfect tend to encourage users to think creatively further and formulate additions or adjustments.

Before the idea implemented in the prototype is tested in the next phase, it makes sense to implement another clear alignment with regard to the question to be tested. A useful approach here can be an idea sketch in which the idea on which the prototype is based is again summarized concisely and to the point. An idea sketch presents the following topics in relation to the described idea:

- The idea
- Sketch of the prototype
- Formulation of the idea
- Target audience and situation in which the prototype / solution approach is to be tested
- What reaction/emotion ... should be triggered by the prototype?

Once the idea and the reaction aimed for with the solution approach have been captured in this way, we can move on to the actual implementation. We move into the test phase with the prototype.

Testing

The final phase of the Design Thinking process is testing. Whereby this does not mean that nothing else could come after testing. Rather, it is very possible that after a testing phase the realization matures that it makes sense to return to an earlier phase, for example to the idea phase, because the ideas developed there did not meet the customer's needs sufficiently. Or we may even go back to the problem area if we have the impression that we should take a closer look at the problem again or narrow it down further. Within the framework of an iterative process model such as design thinking, there is no linear process; instead, we always react to the insights gained and adjust the process and the next steps as needed.

Testing helps us to further expand our perception of the users and their needs. The goal of testing is therefore not primarily that we have already found "THE" solution to the customer's problem, so to speak, in the first run, but that the tested prototype provides us with further insights into the customer's benefits and needs, which form a basis for further improvements and approaches. From my experience, it proves to be very important when "pressure" is taken out of the process in this way. The idea that the first prototype is already "the last word in wisdom" is not goal-oriented and puts both the Design Thinking team and the user under pressure, which tends to prevent innovative solutions or at least makes them more difficult.

Accordingly, it makes sense to get the process through to testing very early on. If prototype testing is tackled relatively late, there is much more pressure to get it all into the production process, whereas early testing gives us scope for improvement and further innovation. The principle of "fail early, fail often" applies as a procedural pattern. To fail early, to derive improvements and additional insights from it, and to move on with it is an important concept for success in the context of design thinking. However, such an approach presupposes a positive error image, in which errors are understood as a natural part of development and learning.

If we want to test, we should in any case first be clear about what we want to learn / find out with a particular test. We therefore determine a test objective. In this context, the question also arises as to what information must be made available to a tester in advance and what additional questions we would like to ask the tester in order to gain additional points of view if necessary.

For the execution of the test it is useful to assign different roles in advance:

- The host guides the tester through the process
- The observer(s) stays in the background and records verbal and nonverbal utterances during the test
- Other people may be needed to contribute to the prototype and help the tester have a proper interaction by moving things around or similar.

In order to gain a better understanding of the tester's perceptions and insights regarding the test object, we ask the tester to think aloud during the test. It is important that we mainly let the tester speak during the test and hold back on utterances in order to influence the tester's experience and insight as little as possible.

After the test, we need to verify what we can learn from it. This may lead us to go back to an earlier step in the process, for example to revise the prototype. We may also find that additional questions and suggestions have arisen in the course of testing that put our own ideas into a different context again and require further attention there. Findings are often summarized in a feedback grid:

- What worked well?
- Where are there opportunities for improvement/needs?
- Are there any new ideas?
- Have any new questions arisen?

On a facilitation wall, the four dimensions are usually arranged in a cross shape and the various team members tell about their findings and record them in key words in the appropriate quadrant on facilitation cards or sticky notes.

Based on the results, the team agrees on the next steps.

CHAPTER THREE

Implementing design thinking in companies

Many companies use Design Thinking because they either already work according to agile approaches or hope to create a first step into the agile world and the advantages beckoning there with Design Thinking. Especially in companies that already work with Scrum or other agile methods and frameworks, Design Thinking seems to be recommended as an innovation generator.

Very different areas of application can be identified. We can roughly divide them into three different areas of innovation:

1. The organization is looking for opportunities to provide additional functionality or offerings - based on the existing portfolio already purchased by the customer, if applicable - for existing customers.
2. The organization is looking for additional new offerings for the existing customers or for potential customers with similar requirements in the existing range of offerings.
3. The organization is looking for new business areas or products in order to address new markets, if necessary.

Design thinking can be used in all areas. However, the questions and possibly also the composition of the corresponding design thinking teams change.

As long as we are in the context of product improvements, design thinking initiatives are often not quite as spectacular and are often not about huge throws, but more about improving what already exists. Results of design thinking challenges in this area are usually associated with very limited risk. You know your customers and can estimate the market potential and potential acceptance based on customer feedback or support cases, for example. However, this also means that design thinking is often not the method of choice in this area, because design thinking tends to focus on rethinking questions and not so much on optimizing existing ones.

If we now think about new products or even new markets, there is also an increased risk that we will make a mistake based on our assumptions and end up with a wonderful solution for a product that many people perceive as a problem, but which is not so decisive or significant for them that they would be willing to spend money or take action for a solution in this regard.

One approach that established companies also like to use to test the market opportunities of a new product is the "lean startup" approach described by Eric Ries.

Lean Startup - a brief introduction

Some companies create new solution ideas and then implement them with a lot of effort. Depending on the problem and the solution, this can take many months or even several years. When they finally reach the market, they discover that the market may not be interested in their solution or that completely different aspects of the solution are of interest to potential customers than the implemented solution offers.

Lean Startup, an approach by Eric Ries, who has written a very readable book on this topic with the same title, takes a completely different approach here. This is based on the Lean Startup cycle "Build - Measure - Learn".

This does not involve planning a huge solution and then implementing it over a long period of time, but rather designing a minimal solution, often also called MVP (Minimal Viable Product), which is mainly intended to clarify market needs and gain feedback on the real needs and wishes of (potential) customers with regard to the envisaged solution. Ideally, this MVP is already suitable for generating initial revenues. However, it may also be that the MVP is designed in a completely different way.

Examples of MVPs could include:

- A website where customers can discuss their needs regarding the product and where, for example, customers can register their interest in the development and news about the product in the form of a subscription to the newsletter.

- A presentation of the project on a platform like Kickstarter or similar, where interested parties can already pre-order a product and with their money the development can be financed.
- For example, some authors post book projects as Kindle books on Amazon and don't start writing until a sufficient number of pre-orders have been received.
- A software solution that first delivers the basic functionality of the planned solution, which is then further developed based on user feedback.

All of the above approaches pursue at least two goals: 1) not to produce anything for which there is no market, and 2) to pursue and continue the (further) development of the product not based on one's own ideas and conceptions, but based on feedback from customers.

In many cases, such developments are not implemented all at once afterwards, but are realized in iterations (repeating development cycles), the content of which is based in each case on the insights received and user feedback. This means that implementations of core topics can be positioned on the market much more quickly than if the entire functionality has to be implemented before a release, and customer needs can be addressed much more precisely, which is an additional advantage in sales. An important advantage is that the risk of investing a lot of money in projects and product developments that the customer does not want is significantly reduced, because without corresponding demand, development can be stopped early and resources can be used for more promising topics.

The approach was originally designed primarily for startup companies to reduce the likelihood of ruining founders who fall in love with "their product", implement it, only to eventually find that there is no market for it. In the meantime, Lean Startup is increasingly being used by global corporations in the context of development, often in combination with other agile approaches.

Lean Startup as the next step after Design Thinking

One may now ask whether Lean Startup is not possibly a Design Thinking alternative or whether Design Thinking and Lean Startup are compatible. In fact, there are of course companies that use only one of the approaches mentioned, sometimes separately or in combination with other approaches. However, more and more companies are also combining the two frameworks very successfully. Two possible approaches can be identified, depending on where the interface and cooperation between the two approaches is defined.

The two approaches can be briefly stated as follows:

- Incorporation of Lean Startup in the "Generate and test prototypes" process step
- Integration of Lean Startup for the development of the solution ideas developed in Design Thinking.

Incorporation of Lean Startup in the "Generate and test prototypes" process step

In the Design Thinking process step "Generate prototypes", very different topics are evaluated by means of prototypes. This often happens in the course of several iterations, in which initially rather smaller elements or questions are checked, so that finally a prototype of the solution/s found in the process is implemented.

This last step in particular is sometimes taken by users with the help of a lean startup MVP approach, in which the prototype is implemented as a minimum viable product and then further developed based on feedback during testing. The advantage of this approach is that in some contexts feedback can already be obtained from a larger user group that might not otherwise have been reached, and that ideally the prototype can already generate initial benefits or even initial revenues.

Integration of Lean Startup for the development of the solution ideas developed in Design Thinking.

If the Lean Startup process is placed downstream of the Design Thinking process, it can be achieved in this way that the innovation process of the Design Thinking model is extended, as it were, by a further process which is based on the same mindset and further ensures that the implemented requirements correspond to the actual wishes of the customers. In this context, one can even go so far as to say that the Lean Startup model interacts with the Design Thinking approach in such a way that, if necessary

- based on experience with the implemented, step-by-step developing solution - partial questions or wishes on the part of the users are in turn developed within the framework of the Design Thinking approach.

Scrum - an introduction

Many books have been written on the agile framework, some of them very detailed, and I am happy to refer to them for an in-depth discussion of this framework. Here, the framework will only be roughly outlined and its key success factors will be highlighted.

Incorrectly, Scrum is often referred to as a project management methodology. This is not the case. Rather, Scrum describes a relatively simple process for developing products. In contrast, many aspects that make up classic project management are not covered by Scrum. The Scrum Guide by Jeff Sutherland and Ken Schwaber describes this as follows:

"The Scrum framework is intentionally incomplete, defining only the parts needed to implement Scrum theory.Scrum builds on the collective intelligence of the people who use it. Rather than giving people detailed instructions, Scrum's rules guide their relationships and interactions.

Various processes, techniques and methods can be used within the framework. Scrum wraps around existing practices or makes them obsolete. Scrum makes visible the relative effectiveness of current management, environment, and work techniques so that improvements can be made."

In Scrum, one or more Scrum teams, each with a maximum of ten people in the roles of "Scrum Master", "Product Owner" and "Developer", develop products in an iterative process. The corresponding iterations, called sprints, each last a maximum of one month. In these sprints, the team's task is to add additional features to the solution for the customer, the selection of which is based on the focus of maximum value creation for the customer. At the end of the iteration - i.e. the development cycle - the Scrum team meets with stakeholders, who are asked to give the team feedback on the features presented in the meeting (Sprint Review). This is not an acceptance of the features, but an event of joint learning in which the experts involved - the Scrum team as the competence team for the implementation and the stakeholders as the competence bearers for the technical requirements - look at what has been achieved together and seek ways to optimize the benefits for the customers.

Based on the feedback and insights of the Scrum team, the next iteration is planned and implemented after the completion of one iteration. The process is carried out as often as necessary until sufficient value has been created for the customer. The goal is thus not to create a solution that is as comprehensive as possible, but one that is as beneficial as possible. Ideally, already completed features (product backlog items) are also released during the development process. This offers the advantage that initial benefits can already be realized and feedback from real users can be obtained, which in turn flows into further planning.

Many users reduce Scrum to a kind of collection of methods for implementing solutions, with most users being based in the IT context. In fact, Scrum's approaches may have some benefit in themselves. However, it must be understood that the real success factor of Scrum - just as of any agile approach - lies in a capable, motivated team that identifies with its task and its goals, gets involved in the development and achieves synergies through teamwork. For this, an environment that promotes this mindset and the corresponding framework conditions are absolutely necessary. Where these are missing, only marginal success can be generated by implementing Scrum processes. Unfortunately, many users do not understand this fact or do not see themselves in a position to take it into account within the framework of their organization. This does not only apply to the use of Scrum, but to all agile methods and frameworks. It is therefore of no use - as many companies are currently doing - to migrate from one agile framework to another because they hope to generate more success there, if they do not also work fundamentally on the framework conditions and corporate mindset. The latter, by the way, does not mean the often prominent buzzwords that some companies present as their maxims and incorporate into their corporate communication in a promotionally effective manner, but rather what is actually lived in everyday corporate life and exemplified by the management.

Scrum, Design Thinking and Lean Startup?

Scrum, Design Thinking and Lean Startup are three of several hundred agile frameworks and methods. They all have a clear scope of application:

- Design Thinking: Innovation Process
- Lean Startup: Product development process based on customer feedback

- Scrum: Product development framework for value-maximized products based on customer feedback

Based on these lines, one might think that Lean Startup and Scrum would be alternatives and that it would make sense to decide whether to use Lean Startup or Scrum. Also, the issue of Scrum working together with Design Thinking has not even been addressed yet. So let us now move forward step by step.

Let's start with the "simpler" combination: Scrum and Design Thinking. In this context, it should be said that we have two completely different purposes of the different approaches here. Design Thinking is about innovation and Scrum is about realization. So the simplest and most common type of combination is that Design Thinking is used to develop a product idea and then from this product idea the requirements are taken into a Scrum product backlog and implemented using Scrum.

Another possible combination is the integration of Scrum in the context of prototype development. In this case, the design thinking team hands over a product idea to the Scrum team, which then implements this idea by taking the first steps towards realizing the idea in a first sprint and then continuously adapting it based on the feedback in the sprint review. In this context it has to be said that Scrum can also be approached as an alternative to Design Thinking by working iteratively on solution ideas based on a question and gradually developing a solution based on the feedback and the learning successes. The reason that this is very rarely done is that there is a perception that too much time of the scarce resource Scrum team is thereby used, while no project with corresponding funding has even been started yet. In short: The positioning of Scrum teams and their integration into the development process is a different process in many companies.

Another possibility of cooperation between Scrum and Design Thinking is that Design Thinking is used within a Scrum process for the development of requirements. This would change the Leading Approach, so to speak. Scrum.org, however, has not only chosen a comparable approach in this very context in combination with Lean UX, but has even included it in the portfolio as its own certification (Scrum.org PSU).

If we now ask ourselves what role Lean Startup can offer in such a combination, the answer is quite simple. Lean Startup is not an approach to managing a product development as a team development process, but focuses on the issue of release management, i.e. mapping what is delivered and in what order based on customer/user feedback. How a development team (in whatever composition) does that is not part of the framework. This is a good fit, since the topic "Release Management" is again not a core topic of Scrum and the corresponding statements in the Scrum Guide are minimal. This results in a very good complement, which is successfully used with or without the combination with Design Thinking by thousands of organizations worldwide.

CHAPTER FOUR

Design Thinking and Leadership

In recent years, many organizations have decided to use design thinking as part of their innovation strategy. In doing so, the question of measurability arises for many organizations. Is design thinking now simply a new fashion trend or is it a sustainable approach? How should effort and benefit be measured? How to justify the corresponding costs and efforts?

In fact, concrete measurability is only possible to a very limited extent. Of course, it is possible to determine the success of products developed with a design thinking initiative, for example. But this does not mean, of course, that a different approach might not have resulted in a product that would have been even more successful. Thus, the "justification" for the use of Design Thinking often results from the simple necessity to find an approach in a constantly changing environment, which is often described with the term "VUCA world" (Volatility-Uncertainty-Complexity-Ambiguity), which can keep pace with this degree of change in viewpoints, technology and markets.

Basically, the use of Design Thinking takes place on different hierarchical levels. There is just as much the product manager, who uses design thinking with his team to further develop existing products in line with the market, as the division or department managers, who use design thinking to rethink markets and challenges and to support their own team with regard to building cooperation and finding synergies. In some cases, however, Design Thinking is also thought of as part of the agilization of an entire company and corresponding initiatives are often initiated by management.

Wherever such initiatives are set up, we always find that they are far less about implementing new techniques in the organization than about making the way we work together more agile. In this context, the research of MIT professor Douglas McGregor from 1960 is particularly worth mentioning. It is often cited with the keywords "X-theory and Y-theory".

Theory X essentially states that employees are lazy and unmotivated and will avoid work as much as possible. They shy away from responsibility and want strong leadership that "takes them by the hand" and sets clear guidelines. Appropriate fulfillment is ensured through strict control and, if necessary, appropriate sanctions.

Theory Y, on the other hand, states that employees are motivated to identify with their work and their employer. Self-responsibility offers an important motivation. For this, employees need an environment in which they can develop and contribute with their skills and knowledge and develop each other in the group. They take responsibility and are innovative. This is because people possess a high degree of imagination, judgment and inventiveness to solve organizational problems.

The exciting message of these two theories is not that there is a "classification" of employees here. On the contrary, the theory says much more about the leader and the organization, because experience shows that leaders and organizations that "believe" in theory X will inevitably also have "theory X employees", while those that have a theory Y worldview will undoubtedly also find corresponding teams. This is not magic, but depends causally on the leadership behavior of the person and/or the organization.

A leader who represents an image of man according to Theory X will consequently instruct his employees in detail and make it clear that deviations will not be tolerated. The employees, in turn, will understand that self-initiative is dangerous. "Service by the book" is the best possible way of acting, and since they themselves do not contribute in any way but essentially act as tools of a thinking boss, little identification with the work or the results achieved is to be expected.

In contrast, in an organization where a Theory Y view of human beings is lived, the supervisor understands the potential that lies within his employees. The best possible approach for him is to provide his team with the resources and the framework to enable them to work optimally, and to share his knowledge and experience with the team only when necessary to support further development. In such an environment, the team will also be a theory Y team. This may take some time if the team has previously experienced a different situation, but with appropriate support, there is a strong likelihood of appropriate development into Theory Y employees.

So what does this mean for the use of design thinking in an organization? Quite simply, if an organization wants to be successful with an approach based on people being innovative and showing a high level of commitment, this will only be achieved if the relevant people also perceive this as part of their reality, i.e. if they are Theory Y employees. This results in a special challenge for the supervisor and the organization surrounding him with regard to the mindset that is lived. A supervisor - at any level - who wants to ensure that a Design Thinking team (and not only this one) delivers maximum benefit and the best possible results must first ask themselves what their own idea of the team is. "What theory do I believe in? What theory do we live in the organization?" Depending on this will reveal the extent to which the organization and supervisor(s) need to work on themselves to create an environment that best supports the use of Design Thinking and the results that come with it.

Success factors for design thinking teams

The question of how Design Thinking teams should be put together arises again and again. Of course, both professional and personal aspects are of great importance.

Design Thinking does not have a specific role model. There are therefore no different roles to which specific responsibilities are tied. Nevertheless, it is important that a Design Thinking process is moderated by a person who has the relevant experience. Some teams use special Design Thinking coaches for this purpose, others select a person from the team who is to design the process accordingly. Although there are now various training providers and certifiers who award Design Thinking titles, it is definitely less a matter of using a person with the "right title" than of having appropriate experience with the process and an empathetic collaboration with the team.

With regard to the composition of the team, professional aspects undoubtedly play a very important role. The goal in the composition of a Design Thinking team is always that the most diverse points of view and competencies are represented. In doing so, it will hardly be possible to use literally all points of view and competencies, but a goal-oriented selection must be made.

In practice, one often very successful approach to putting together teams is to advertise corresponding projects or challenges and invite employees to apply for them. On the one hand, this can reveal aspects that might otherwise have been overlooked, and on the other hand, it can also increase the likelihood of commitment to a topic on the part of the people involved. A good possibility for the final selection is that the applicants are told the general conditions and asked to make a proposal for a team from their ranks (based on the mentioned general conditions such as team size, necessary inclusion of certain areas, etc.). It may be necessary to look for additional resources (internal or external) if they are needed and no one has applied. Often, the best ideas about who else is needed for the team come from the team itself anyway. The corresponding process should be moderated by a person with design thinking experience.

The advantage of such an approach is that, on the one hand, the most important success factor - interest and motivation - can be ensured. In addition, such an approach also offers the advantage, which should not be underestimated, that innovation is perceived by employees as a task and responsibility of the entire team and the entire company and not as the activity of an exclusive, small circle of innovators.

There are also other possibilities for the composition of design thinking teams. As a general rule, approaches in which a leader (whether supervisor or otherwise) assigns employees to such a task tend to be less successful than those in which teams are formed. It may be that the process takes longer. However, it must be made clear anyway that design thinking is not normally aimed at producing solutions as quickly as possible, but rather has a long-term mission.

In some organizations, dedicated design thinking teams exist for certain topics. This certainly has the advantage that the team processes that are usually particularly important in agile constellations (cf. Tuckman: Forming-Storming-Norming-Performing) are less important. However, in my view, these approaches are only useful to a limited extent for two reasons. On the one hand, one can of course ask whether a standard team offers the right personnel for all issues or whether it offers suitable solutions for some issues but does not have the required competencies or experience in other cases and thus only delivers standard solutions and no innovative top performance. Much more important, however, is the message that is sent to the outside world. Instead of supporting innovation and further development as broadly as possible and making it a central corporate topic, it is delegated to a small, exclusive circle. This cannot be in the interests of an organization that wants to play an important, leading role in the future.

Although not part of the design thinking team, equally important to its success is the role and involvement of leadership. It is crucial for the success of Design Thinking teams that their terms of reference are internally known and valued as important. This is the only way to ensure that team members have sufficient resources and are not pulled away by hierarchical superiors when needed or are so busy that there is no energy and time available for creative work. It is equally important that a person with the appropriate position also performs a certain protective function and allows the team to work even if results take a little longer or other unforeseeable situations arise.

CHAPTER SIX

Establishment and development of design thinking teams

Building and developing one or more Design Thinking teams should not stand as a local measure within an organization. Rather, the implementation of such teams, just like the establishment of Scrum teams or other agile teams, is always part of a larger movement. Only in this way can a corresponding measure also be target-oriented and effective.

Accordingly, an agile transformation is important for the entire organization. Only when framework conditions are created or have already been created that encourage employees to identify with their work, their products, and their employer can agile methods and approaches also unfold their effect. Innovation, creativity and commitment cannot be commanded. They emerge from an environment where people identify with what they do, and where their natural interest in being successful and optimizing things is supported and encouraged. In addition, there is a mindset that is geared towards reviewing procedures, products and ways of thinking and looking for improvement. This requires an experimental approach in which alternatives are tried out, verified and then either implemented or discarded. Errors will also occur in the process. Because that is a natural part of experimentation: Not all of them are successful. But if mistakes are now perceived as bad and rejected and - as is unfortunately the case in some companies - more time is spent looking for culprits than on learning from mistakes, then no agile measure will be successful.

In one of his presentations, Simon Sinek describes a situation that occurs far too often in business: employees are laid off in response to poor quarterly figures. This often happens not because there is nothing for the employees to do or because certain skills or knowledge of the relevant people are no longer needed, but primarily because it is intended to show the shareholders that - even if you are generating less revenue - you will still ensure profitability in the future because you are also reducing a corresponding cost block. This measure undoubtedly places fewer demands on management than ensuring that the revenue side improves, and can therefore be seen as a kind of liberating blow.

Now let's change the perspective: How does it feel for the employee who comes home in the evening and has to explain to his or her family that he or she is going to lose his or her job, not because he or she has done something wrong, but because the company has not achieved its goals and one person in his or her department has been cut? From the company's point of view, but perhaps even more important is the question of what signal this sends to the employees who are not being laid off. The measure taken sends them the signal that - if the figures are still not achieved - they may be laid off. This leads to uncertainty and reduces identification with an employer who obviously does not care about the fate of his employees. Some will possibly leave the company, others will do everything not to attract attention, i.e. not to give any reason to be unaffected by the next staff cut. Not making mistakes, not admitting weaknesses ... companies that act this way will not achieve an innovation-friendly basic attitude. Rather, employees in an innovation team will also drive with the handbrake on, so to speak, and "on the safe side". Great successes and innovations can hardly be achieved in this way, and this can naturally lead to a lack of further success, because in this way one tends to only chase after the competition. A number of organizations have recognized this and are trying to achieve this by spinning off small innovation cells. Although this can lead to new products locally, it will not lead to a company as a whole changing in such a way that it can survive in the long term in a constantly changing world characterized by high complexity.

An agile mindset cannot simply be commanded or started at the push of a button. Rather, it is a longer-term process that must be gone through step by step. Ideally, this process is designed as an agile process, although it also makes sense to support such a change by means of classic change management measures (see, for example, Kotter's 8 steps or similar).

Agile development means that the first step is to develop a vision of the future state that is shared by all stakeholders. Subsequently, a first step towards the implementation of the vision is jointly defined and the corresponding measures are implemented. Corresponding steps should take place in very clear time frames. 1-2 months should be the maximum in order to keep the energy in the process. At the end of the time, it is evaluated together what was done and if the planned goal was reached. What was successful is kept and what did not work is discarded. Based on the experience gained together and the results achieved, the next step is jointly defined and again implemented. In this way, the team develops step by step in the direction of agility.

Of course, implementation in larger organizations will be more complex. Here, too, a shared vision of the organization is of great importance. It goes without saying that it is important that the corresponding vision does not represent a marketing statement, but an actual goal. It must be represented and exemplified by the top management. Only then is implementation feasible. Subsequently, it may very well be that different units, divisions or departments set goals for themselves individually, all of which are steps in the direction of the common vision. These can be implemented iteratively in these areas as described above. In such structures, it is always important that appropriate coordination also takes place here across the various hierarchy levels, and above all that an understanding of the importance of synergies is developed. It is of no use if one department achieves goals ... it is rather always about a change of the entire organization. Only then can goals be achieved. Accordingly, any silo goals and considerations are nonsensical. Methods such as OKR can be very helpful with regard to such implementations.

Based on the measures taken to agilize the company, the use of agile methods and frameworks is also indicated. Here, too, it makes sense not to start from big-bang approaches, but to jointly define goals and approach them step by step. The use of retrospectives, i.e. events in which progress in collaboration is considered and the next measures are discussed and planned with regard to achieving a common goal, are part of every agile initiative, whether it is about the agilization of a company or the implementation of an agile method such as Design Thinking or a framework such as Scrum.